Grave Unknown

A Poetry Collection written by
Ruby Wednesday

Printed in the United Kingdom

First Printing, 2022

ISBN 978-1-6780-0481-1

@mxrubywednesday

rubywednesday.bandcamp.com

patreon.com/mxrubywednesday

In memory of
Allen Stalley and
Alan and Della Stacey

Thank you for showing me so many beautiful things.

Acknowledgments

These past few years have been absolutely crazy for a lot of us, so much has happened and so much has changed; yet there have been a few people that have continued to support me and stick by my side.

I want to thank you for continuing the faith, the momentum and for keeping the dream very much alive.

I must start with my incredible parents, Andrew and Jacqueline. Thank you for being my biggest fans. Your constant support, encouragement and patience with everything I threw your way has meant the world to me. My brothers did pretty alright too.

To my friends, you are few yet you are mighty. I'd like to thank a few of you in particular whom I really could not have done any of this without.

Russell, I'd be completely lost without you. I can't believe you've stuck by me for this long. I feel incredibly honoured to be your friend, and to be able to create beautiful things with you is a true gift.

Alisa, your faith in my abilities is pretty astounding and I'm incredibly grateful for your relentless reassurance.

Maxim, none of this would've happened unless I had you on one of my shoulders spurring me on; which shoulder you may decide.

Amelia, because I'd be really screwed if I didn't have someone to talk Tarot with, challenge my perspective and hype me up.

I must also thank Rose Thorne and Benjamin Louche for believing in my work. For reading bits over, giving feedback and being so incredibly helpful with this particular process and beyond. Also, for introducing me to Jon Attfield who gifted me the notepad that I wrote these poems in. Thank you, Jon, for lending your talents for the cover art; I love it.

I never really understood the immense power of community until we were all locked inside. I was suddenly left with nothing and when I started reading Tarot on Instagram Live sessions through jetlagged delirium, it was the people who joined me that gave me a small glimmer of purpose; you made me value myself and, more importantly, my work.

My patrons, you're absolutely wonderful and I hope you enjoy this book now that it's *finally* with us. Not only have you been an incredible support system but you have kept my love of Tarot burning which I think is one of the most important things.

Finally, to my dearest, Laura Groves.
You are a constant inspiration. I can't even begin to imagine where to start in describing my gratitude for your very existence. From cooked breakfasts to roast dinners, from laughter to tears, true crime documentaries, sometimes questionable film choices and especially *Celebrity Ghost Stories* and *Bullseye*.
Thank you for your openness, your wisdom, your intuition and, of course, all of the music.
And the endless cups of coffee.

o

Gifted

For the fools
Still searching for moments
Of magic

I

Sleight of Hand

Slick, sharp blades
Tumble from your bloodied tongue
Falling into a haphazard pile
In my cupped hands

Beautiful words scrawled
Upon each tiny mirror
In romantic cursive,
Crimson ink

There is a power in you
That terrifies me
There is a power in you
That repulses me

We all have an ability
And we all have a devilry
That chews, that devours
In our own personal abyss

Though
It is our decision
Which one we allow
To consume us

II

Passing of the Scripture

Knelt before your gracious silence
Waves lapping at your delicate shores
Salted air stinging my tear-filled eyes
With ruby fruit cradled in my hands

Honed fingernails piercing the waxy flesh
Liquor bleeding into the creases of my palms
Tearing through bloodied tendrils
Forcing fistfuls of seeds into my salivating mouth

The corner of your lip curls slowly upward
I look upon you; though my face reflects
With wry smile gazing back
Smothered in garnet-stained juice

III

Forty-Nine Days

Brittle limbs, a snapped body
Quiet decomposition amongst
The undergrowth
Consumed by nettles, fern and thorn

Peaceful and fading
Serene and waning

In the damp
Hungry spores breed
Take root and expand; viral
Spreading gracefully

Consuming life, becoming life
A silent rotted burst of being
From the decay. Warm, moist decay
That chews rapidly through flesh

Released and formed
Slain and abolished

Through this fallen Silver Birch
The meek mycelium breeds
Sprouting polypore, shank and bonnets
Silent deterioration burst into blooming caps

There is new life after death
There is new life within death

IV

The First Son

A delicately steaming black coffee
Presented in porcelain cup and saucer
A perfect tarry blend of bitter sweetness
An appreciative exhale from the first
Blackened sip; tendrils of breath curling
From my throat and my tongue content

And you.
Your perfectly placed, poised posture
Behind open grand piano; secure, strong, square
You play the greats, some contemporaries,
Meandering through humid summer Iris gardens
And ponder upon things to work on

A cigarette hissing in a leaf-shaped ashtray
The sunlight piercing through the glass doors
Catching a singular blue-tinted stream of smoke
Curling toward the ceiling
Harsh against the searing, pink lilies
Rivalling your morning grapefruit

Abandoned Malbec litters the room and
I gaze upon last night's rouge port
Rhythmically oscillate inside a slight chalice
As you strike keys, I place a kiss upon your crown
Running my fingers through your hair
Your beard and across your chest

Opened mouthed and opened eyed kisses
And suddenly, I am not so secure
I feel I miss you already
Or an idea at least.

V

Pedagogue

Youth, Father and Sage
Bathe in your worship as you sleep, child
Whilst Maiden, Mother and Crone dwindle
Yet wait for you patiently, child
Waiting to welcome you home

Your teachers are lying to you, child
You must consume their knowledge
You must hear and you must listen to everything,
Of utmost importance, child
Question that and
Question them
You must question what you are reading right now, child
Question every single word that you read
Every utterance that you hear
The grandeur is to tempt you from the doorway
To distract you from the keys, child

Youth, Father and Sage
Bathe in your worship as you sleep, child
Whilst Maiden, Mother and Crone dwindle

VI

Taken by a Dropped Surprise

Taken by a dropped surprise
Tension on my neck, as I
Am informed of a great escape
My mouth engulfed with bitter taste

The creases sit around the eyes
However much that you despise
The constant state of belligerence
Left a pool of abandoned compliments

Upon the furrowed brow I sit
A soft connection from dry lips
Like the one upon your neck
Fractions of skin that I inspect

The brief moments that will sit with me
Will be the ones where it was seen
At that tenderness of crumbled walls
A confession, where the words would fall

Tumbled from the very teeth
That once kept those secrets safe and deep
A subtle pain where my head will sit
That same place where so did my lips

VII

Amore Armour

My defences were once impervious
And I was once so delicate inside.
That shield has slipped now
My outsides feel somewhat vulnerable

My armour weakened
My skin peeled away
Where the tiniest of breezes
Prickle the exposed nerves

My exterior discarded
And now we must wait
In order for this new sheath to crystallise
Keeping you out, keeping me in

Perhaps then I can continue
Continue to venture, to stray
Uncover somewhere new,
Though for now,
We are brittle and we are hiding.

VIII

Give Me Strength

Give me the strength
To pull back the bedsheets and expose my pallid skin to the
cool air

Give me the strength
To dress and lumber my body to the kitchen to make the first
coffee

Give me the strength
To resist smoking unnecessary cigarettes

Give me the strength
To stop zombie-like scrolling; staring into haunted screens

Give me the strength
To answer when the phone rings

Give me the strength
To not break my silence toward him

Give me the strength
To not look at old photographs
And reminisce over good times with bad people

Give me the strength
To feed my body

Give me the strength
To only take the suggested dose

Give me the strength
To shower, brush my teeth,
Feel a fresh breeze caress my lungs

Give me the strength
To not break my silence toward him
Again

Give me the strength
To not lose control and keep the cracks from breaking open

Give me the strength
To not push the intolerable in front of traffic or trains
Or myself even

Give me the strength
To not cry in front of these strangers

Give me the strength
To smile at the appropriate people

Give me the strength
To look at a to-do list and not be overwhelmed
By the smog in my mind

Give me the strength
To not jump

Give me the strength
To keep my eyes open whilst crossing roads

Give me the strength
To get out of bed

IX

Singing to an Empty Room

A single red light
In an otherwise vacuous darkness
Inspect your palms
Watch your folding fingers
Study the creases carved into the flesh

A hollow wind groaning through
A copious vacancy
The longing heartbreak for no one
Grief seared into your breast
The sadness, the absence

Is anyone out there?
Am I singing to an empty room?
Even these self-indulgent passages
Left folded and unread
Pressed inside these pages

X

Logarithm

Our time is not linear, friend
The face of a clock is no two-dimensional circle
Time is cyclical, yes
Only from the perspective in which we perceive it

We, in truth, stare into a gateway
Into a tunnel of time
Not a circle; we stare into a continuous spiral
The hands will wind around the image
And return to a point that appears original

That time is no longer yours
We have progressed through this time
Further into the tunnel
We're on a new rung of this spiral

We have endured
We have suffered
We have grown
We have aged

This time only seems to exist
Because of the existence of our demise.

XI

To Lady Justice

Cast your blindfold eyes
Across the city
With back turned upon Saint Paul
Grasping on to diplomacy and reality
Evermore faced from the dogmatic production of
A crucifix-lecherous boys' club
Remaining impartial to the
Falsehoods of the church
And now, Themis,
I fear it is too late
I fear you have turned your back on us all

XII

Diamond Rain

Today I saw where a man's last moments occurred
Stray creepers crawled inside his shed
Through the cracks underneath the door
Searching for the one who nurtured them
Reaching up to the ceiling to pull him down
Release a trapped soul from its confines

An upturned mug, to me
The most harrowing souvenir
The passing of durational chaos, a torturous struggle
A trusty companion, quenching thirst
As he would look upon his land
Across his kingdom
Perhaps the only thing he felt he had left

I wonder
If the flowers fear their inevitable demise
If the plants feel it time for them to cease
I am, of course, aware that it is cyclical
But we fear the end of ours, do we not?
I wonder if they have an awareness
Knowledge of the approach of
Their end
And if they were to mourn
When Death has swept by

XIII

I met you once, briefly

Amongst the bleak stillness
I stare into what was once a recognisable face
Perhaps not so dissimilar to my own
Or, maybe, there was never a time before
Born promptly in to death

It's quiet here
I can see why you may like it
It must be pleasant here for you
As the breeze whips around
The fabric draped around your frame
Whistling through empty eye sockets
I wonder what we're doing here

Occasionally we will join
And every so often, I think you appear to show
A moment of what's to come
To stare Death in the face, though
Death doesn't look back
So, neither should we

XIV

Mother's Return

The putrefying waters
That we have pissed in
The Mother intoxicated with
Poisons that we cast into her

Kept inebriated, kept submissive
She must not sober
She must remain half-cut
And subservient

If she were to sober
The rivers will begin to flow backward
Waterfalls will begin to climb
Back up the mountainside

The oceans drained
The life below suffocated
Leaving vast barren gashes in the earth
Where the Seven Seas once danced and raged

No more flowers
No more fruit
No more meat
No more

One of these days
She will take it back
The day the rivers begin to flow backward

XV

Narcissist's Puppet

The bruising around my throat from the noose of chains
Wrenching me back into position if I would wander
Wrists worn raw and bleeding from incessant blind puppetry
Whilst you remind me to love myself and
To not accept mistreatment from the wretched world
To be relentlessly and unapologetically myself;
To an extent
Yet, when the mask slips
And I see what lurks behind
It was you
All along, it was you
You were the beast, the Wizard
I see these chains are loose
These chains were always loose
Knowing I could've left at any moment
Abandoned you in your own twisted darkness
Your words, your curses and self-indulgence
That incarcerated me
Enslaved by serpent silver-tongued deceit
Your aching hunger for superiority
Importance, adoration, devotion
I understand
I understand that I had my uses to you
Just another sentient doll stuffed with voice box
Crammed with what you yearned to hear
Full of strenuous, relentless doting words
For you to pull, release and revel in manipulated praise
The batteries now long dead

And no matter the nuanced exploitations
Tactics of brute-like threats built from suppressed rage
So quick to switch to bargaining when the former would fail
Fortunately, that person you once knew is long dead
I buried them myself

XVI

Plummet into the Dark

So full of fear
We are all so full of fear
The *unknown* being what we are truly afraid of

Something we do not, cannot comprehend
Something we fail to get our heads wrapped around

The breeze whips through my hair
As I stare toward the ground below me
From my window over the treetops and beyond
I am not afraid of the falling
I am not afraid of the brief flying freedom
It is beyond that freedom; what comes after

If I were to shift my weight
Let go of the carpet at my feet
And teeter through the glass
I would soar
I would soar to the ground
Strike the earth like lightning
Smashing straight through the concrete
Passing the dirt, the filth, the worms, the dead
Continue into an unknown beyond
Somewhere quiet and painless
Or somewhere torturous and violent
Or nothing
Endless nothing

Human megalomania
Creating a pointless afterward
An obsessive narcissistic compulsion
That our selves must continue

So full of fear
We are all so full of fear

XVII

Follow

Look toward the blue-black sky
The vastness of unfathomable space
The vastness of lost time; dead time
Between you, between us, between them

Lay for a humbling moment
Watch Sirius scorch and drift
Amongst the fields of the evening
Orion calling after him during the hunt

XVIII

Lunar Archer

The silver rays of the Harvest Moon
Flood into the corners of my bedroom
You are quick to chase your brother this time of year
As you dance around us
Painting spirographs across the Heavens
Ensnaring the Earth in a cosmic spiderweb

I'll leave my curtains pulled open for you
I have no desire to prevent you
From visiting during and beyond
The twilight hours. Please,
Protect me as I slumber; slay the sprites
That toy with my dreams until your brother's return

XIX

Solar Archer

As golden and as radiant as you are
Cradling lyre and quiver crowded with divine quarrel
Bewitching my mind, wound my soul
Filling me with poetry, music and
Gifts of sight beyond human means

A soft scent of hyacinth lingers from your pores
I kiss a golden tear that slowly trickles
Down your marbled face
Fingernails caress your scalp to your nape
You pull closer and our lips would meet
Entwined within you; still and radiant

Amongst woodland whispers
Energetic conversation between you and I
And the life around us, striving to obtain connection
For us to feel less abandoned within the spaces between
My gratitude to the archer, in hopes I too remain

XX

Return

What are you doing here, boy?

I put you in the fucking ground
And left you behind
For good reason

XXI

A Choice

Calm your mind here
It is never truly over

We can begin again
Whenever we need

We have an eternity here

Turn your insides out and
Welcome the transcendent syzygy

Steal moments to dance with yourself
With every aspect of yourself, your selves

You have permission
Take it with you, or start again

About the author

Ruby Wednesday is an artist, performer and writer in London. Growing up in the South West of England, Ruby aspired to leave the confines of a small town and escape to the Big Smoke.

After studying a Foundation Diploma in Art and Design, they left home and attended Wimbledon College of Art where they explored many aspects of the self through performative works of photography, sculpture and writing. Throughout their practice, they began to explore their inner relationship exploring their gender identity and began to find a sense of belonging within the queer community by attending cabaret shows around London.

Beginning their professional performing career in burlesque, drag and queer performance, Ruby has performed internationally alongside writing their debut album 'Narcissus' with lifetime friend and collaborator, Russell Lanigan.

'Narcissus' is a concept album inspired by the occult, the exploration of self, relationships and our connections to the Universe. Bringing together musical influences from shoegaze, post-punk and alternative indie rock with melodic guitar, haunting synth and lyrical vocals, the album stitches together blinks of existence that leave lasting impressions and connect many of us through our experiences.

Ruby Wednesday has been performing in the Cabaret & Queer scene nationally and internationally for over a decade including Glastonbury Festival, the legendary House of Yes in Brooklyn and at the Adelaide Fringe collaborating with New York based collective, 'Blunderland'.

This is their first published work of poetry.

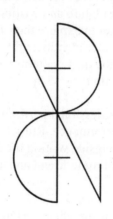